Recovering from the Loss of a Love

H. NORMAN WRIGHT

D1560306

AspirePress

Torrance, California

AspirePress

Contents

CHAPTER ONE

Breakup Blues

"Let's just be friends." Have you ever heard those fateful words? Or how about "I think it would be better if we stopped seeing each other"? Heartbreak, disappointment, loneliness, numbness—these are our feelings when we experience a broken relationship.

One of the greatest delights in life is loving another person, but one of the greatest disappointments in life is being in love with a person who neither loves you nor wants to be a part of your life any longer. In addition, every survivor of a broken relationship is haunted by the residue of fear about future relationships. The trauma of a lost love is one of life's most painful hurts, and anxiety about loving again is one of life's greatest fears.

THE IMPACT OF HEARTBREAK

The initial response to the breakup of a relationship is often a sense of unreality. *This must be happening to someone else. It couldn't be happening to me.* Some have said they felt as if they were frozen in time. Everything just stood still. Others have said they actually pinched themselves, because it was like a bad dream or a nightmare: they just wanted to wake up and discover it wasn't real.

If the loss was intense, you might feel numb for a couple of days, and then the intensity of all the emotions will hit. For some, the devastation and intensity of emotions isn't much different from that of experiencing the death of a close friend or family member.

The first few days after a breakup are sometimes referred to as the *impact phase*. When two cars hit each other, an impact occurs. And you know the result of that—damage. Similarly, the "damage" (pain) you experience after a breakup will depend on the length and intensity of the relationship and on your reluctance to have it end.

A female client in her early thirties explained:

> It feels as though I was driving along a nice residential street in a new car and all of a sudden someone backed out of a driveway and just blindsided me. Not only that, they didn't stop to see what damage they did. They just hit me and drove off. So I'm left to deal with the damage all by myself. I feel victimized.

If your ex-partner has just broken up with you, you probably long for the relationship you once had. For some, this longing becomes an obsession dominating every waking moment. Nothing has meaning until the relationship is restored, but restoration of the relationship exactly as it was happens very infrequently.

What Reactions Are Normal?

What's the initial week after the breakup typically like? Any of the following may happen:

> ➢ You may have difficulty concentrating. Your mind returns to the relationship and you replay the events again and again.

- You may stay by the phone and your computer, waiting for a call, a text, or an e-mail.

- You may listen to sad songs and personalize them.

- You may either spend time making plans for getting the person back or focusing on why it's best you're not in the relationship anymore.

- You may rehearse events and conversations to determine what went wrong and what you could have done or said differently.

- You may recall the good times and wonder if any of the positive statements your ex-partner made were true.

- You may focus on what you could do differently—such as dressing more stylishly or being more sensitive to draw him or her back.

- You may concentrate on only the positive experiences and blank out the bad times.

- You may think that surely you could have done something to avoid this breakup. Guilt is likely to be your constant companion whether it's warranted or not.

➤ You may think of ways to get even or make your ex-partner feel the same pain as you do.

In heartbreak, it's not just a heart that is shattered but a dream as well. It feels as though your life has been stopped cold. You're sitting there holding the pieces of your heart in your hands, and time is moving forward while leaving you in its wake. And the more life moves on, the more you feel as if you can never catch up. You're in a state of painful suspended animation. One of my young male clients told me:

I wish I could quit thinking about her. We went together for three years. I just assumed we'd get married. What I got instead was dumped. I never knew I could feel this bad. I feel like I'm going through a divorce, but at least divorced people have recovery groups to help them. There's nothing for me. I wake up and there she is—sitting in my thought life, taking over the day. I wish there was an anti-memory pill.

Unfortunately, there's no such pill. You remember the good times as well as the hurts and the mistakes, and each memory activates pain.

The pain is intensified by the feeling that no one else really understands. The grief you feel because of this loss in your life can be as intense as a loss by death, but you don't have the support of others as you do when someone dies. No one sends you a card or brings over a meal. You're wounded by the comments and lack of understanding of others. Some chide you with "I told you so" or "You should have seen the problem coming." Others push you, saying, "Get on with your life" or "There are plenty of others out there and better than what you had." All these comments hurt. They don't help.

If depression is now part of your life, expect its symptoms to be with you for a while. Difficulties with sleeping, eating, lack of interest, lethargy, neglect, tears, anger, a negative outlook on life—these are normal responses to loss.

Whether you have lost someone because of death, divorce, or a breakup, sometimes it's helpful to think of all the pain and trauma as one big "ball of grief." This is helpful for two reasons: it helps you put a label on what you are experiencing, and it also normalizes what you're feeling. It's not wrong to experience this jumbled pile of emotions; it's normal. What you're going through is no different from what others experience when going through a similar set of circumstances.

> It's not wrong to experience this jumbled pile of emotions; it's normal.

Some of the men and women who hurt the most are those who are still deeply attached to former spouses or to people to whom they were engaged, and they want their relationships to be restored. They feel desperate, totally out of control, and willing to do almost anything to keep their partners. But they have no control over the decisions of those they love. Being out of control in any situation is fearful, but having no control over a broken relationship is worse. Watching your loved one slip away without any recourse leaves you feeling empty and helpless. You feel as if you're unraveling emotionally.

Why Does It Hurt So Much?

Why do these broken relationships hit us so hard? Part of the happiness in a close, loving relationship comes from being loved by the other person. Consider the parent-child relationship. Usually it is a two-way love relationship. If one of your parents dies of old age, you know that parent didn't die because he or she stopped caring for you. He or she simply died, and you accept that. Similarly, when a pet dies, you realize it wasn't because your pet didn't care for you.

But a breakup in a relationship is different. The love and care that once existed for you has dried up. It's vanished into thin air. But the other person still exists. You may still see each other from time to time, and the frequent reminder of the past makes the breakup even more difficult to handle.

What Are the Secondary Losses?

As you experience the loss of this relationship, at first you experience the absence of the person. But every loss carries with it a series of secondary losses as well—the sense of belonging, and the emotional and practical support. And each of these must be identified, grieved over, and in some way let go. Think of the various losses you've experienced:

➤ The couple relationship (The activities you shared are gone.)

➤ All the rituals you did together—like daily text messages, phone calls, or weekend date night (All those rituals are gone. And you feel the emptiness.)

➤ The comfort and closeness you created

➤ The warmth and affection reflected in the other's eyes

➤ The feelings of having this person as a part of your life

➤ Your hopes and dreams for the future

➤ The members of your partner's family with whom you bonded

➤ Gifts or affirmations you were accustomed to receiving

➤ The emotional and practical support you received on a regular basis

Often when you start a romantic relationship, you leave some of your single friends behind. It may not have been intentional, but it just happened as you invested more time and energy in the new relationship. You may not have thought about it much, because it took place gradually as you experienced the delight of a new love. You were also entering your partner's world and making new friends. Your world became more and more of a couple's world.

But when the relationship ends, you're likely to feel a huge secondary relationship loss. The newly acquired friends may not linger, so you're left with a void. Some of them may feel torn. You may have really clicked with some of them, but their initial loyalty is with your ex. What's more, the friends you had back when you were single may have forgotten about you.

Often, in the aftermath of a breakup, one's vision is so clouded that it's difficult to see the many different losses. But because of each of these losses needs to be grieved over, it's important to identify them.

THE LENGTH OF THE PAIN[1]

Norm, how long? How long is this pain going to last? How long is it going to take for me to recover? When will the thoughts, the feelings, the memories go away, so I can go on with my life? I hear these questions frequently, because I work with many people who are experiencing grief over the loss of a relationship.

I'm not sure I can give you an exact answer, because the estimates vary. We do know, however, that when you lose a close loved one in what is called a "natural" death, the average length of time for recovery is about two years. With an "accidental or caused" death, it's three years, depending upon the circumstances.

The relationship experts who wrote *Letting Go*, a book about recovering from a broken heart, concluded that the average amount of time it takes for haunting memories to subside and for normal functioning to return was usually one half the duration of the relationship. This conclusion was based on interviews with people who also suffered from a loss of self-esteem, depression, and feelings of inadequacy after the breakup. Their finding indicates it would take two years to recover from the loss of a four-year relationship, six years to recover from the loss of a twelve-year relationship, and so on. But the authors also say that the length of recovery time will vary according to the individual and the intensity of the relationship.[2]

Another pair of authors describes the emotional state of people who break up as "love shock," which is a mixture of numbness, disorientation, emptiness, and anxiety. It is similar to a crisis reaction or grieving over any kind of loss. They suggest it takes most people about a year to complete their "love shock" experience, but it's not unusual for the process to take longer.[3]

Here's a good rule of thumb: the more you learn how to cope with crisis and the more knowledgeable you are about grief, the faster you will be able to recover. Learning about grief and realizing that what you're experiencing

You and your grief can't be pushed.

is normal can lift some of your discomfort. And remember, don't try to go through this experience by yourself. We recover better when another person walks with us on the path of recovery.

You and your grief can't be pushed. There's no fast-forward button. You'll recover in stages with some periods of calm in between periods of anxiety. Stabilizing your life involves acceptance of the fact that your life as you knew it for the last year or two or three will never be the same again. It also involves realizing that regardless of how you feel, you have a full life before you—a life full of purpose and meaning.

THE REACTIONS OF FRIENDS AND FAMILY

Recovering from your loss will be a struggle, and you probably won't have the support that you want at this time. You may understand that your recovery will take time, even months, but many of those around you won't be patient with you. They'll prod you with questions and statements to get you back into the mainstream of life.

I know of one couple who broke up after six years. For them, the breakup was a mutual decision with a minimal amount of pain. But it was a different story for their respective families and friends. They were all stunned: it was their lives that came to a standstill, and they gave the couple a lot of grief over the breakup. One female client said about her friends and family:

> I felt as though I'd been excommunicated by life. After four years my ex and I weren't going anywhere. Jim was so nice and likeable, but if we'd married, I would be the initiator and he'd follow. I didn't want to be a mother to my husband. But the

reaction from our friends! It's as though I've got leprosy. He was so close to our boss at the company, I wonder if I've even got a job anymore!

Hopefully some close friends will listen to you and help you through your journey of grief, but well-meaning friends can also give you bad advice. Unfortunately, people love to give advice, even when they really don't know what they're talking about. Why? Because people really do want to help, and they want to feel valued. Most, however, won't give you good advice, because they simply don't know the answers.

Be careful what you ask your friends. It doesn't help to ask them why they think the breakup happened. How would they know? They don't have all the facts, and they do not understand all the dynamics involved. Don't ask them what you should do or how to get the person back in your life. And remember, your friend are friends, not experts.

Often the breakup comes as a major shock to friends and family because while a couple is together, they often do their best to present a rosy picture of how things are between them. It's no surprise, then, that family members and friends are taken off guard when what they thought was a peaceful union suddenly goes up in smoke.

Realignments will occur. Some friends will support your ex; others will support you. The advantage is with the initiator of the breakup here, because he or she has more of an opportunity to develop a support network. But the person who was on the receiving end of the breakup will need to develop a support network as well. The initiator has usually planned his or her steps in advance and the shock response is much less. This is one of the reasons why it's always important to have good friends outside of a romantic relationship.[4]

THE FEAR OF LOVING AGAIN

Some people face breakups squarely, learn from them, override their fears, and grow to trust and love again. But others allow their emotional wounds to remain open; they give in to their fears by withdrawing from any future romantic relationships or by becoming very selective.

Nancy, a thirty-two-year-old, described to me how she felt:

Jim and I dated for two years. I really thought it was going somewhere. We'd had some discussions about the future. We even mentioned marriage. One day we were a couple; the next I was single. There's so much I miss now. I miss his presence. He was enjoyable to have around. And we had a fairly regular pattern of seeing one another and doing things together. It was an enjoyable routine. And I thought we fit together fairly well.

We were mentioned always as a couple. I'm not the only one shocked and upset over this breakup. My friends start to refer to us as a couple and then end up correcting themselves. It's embarrassing for all of us. I'm struggling with a lot, even with figuring out who I really am.

If I only had to deal with the feelings of this breakup it would be a bit easier. But I've had two others. I thought I'd gotten over those all right. But that pain came back as well. So now I'm a third-time loser. Either I have the gift of picking the wrong men, or I pick the right ones and they see defects in me that I'm blind to. Could I have been too cautious in this relationship, because of the other experiences? I don't know. I just don't want this to happen again.

The fear that this could happen again is especially strong if there have been numerous breakups over the years. Once an intimate relationship ends, a part of you wants to try again with a new relationship. But as with Nancy, another part says: "Forget it. Don't do it! It isn't worth the risk!" You're afraid the past will recur, and a new relationship will end up the same way. Or you're afraid you will always feel the loss and pain of your previous breakup and will never be able to reach out and love again.

The fear of reliving the past paralyzes the normal process of building a new relationship. This fear creates a hesitation to invest energy, love, and transparency in a new love interest. Many people who are afraid to move ahead in a new relationship are also afraid to remain behind without anyone to love. They feel trapped between the fear of loving again and the fear that they will never be loved again.

Additional emotions feed the fear of loving again. One of them is guilt—the feeling that you have failed yourself, your ideals, your Lord, or the other person. Sometimes you think, *I wasted all these years on that person.* This guilt may exist even if you were the rejected person. Unresolved guilt damages self-esteem, and low self-esteem produces greater fear. If you feel guilty about a broken relationship, it's important to identify whether the feelings are based on reality (such as breaking a commitment or acting irresponsibly toward the other person) or imagination (taking the blame for something that was not really your responsibility).[5]

If you've experienced a lot of rejection in your life, your fear of being rejected again could cause you to behave in ways that bring about rejection. And many people are so down on themselves that they're their own worst enemies. They put themselves down, degrade themselves, dump on themselves, and rarely give themselves the benefit of the doubt. And since they don't like themselves, they project a negative picture of who they are to others.

But your concern now may be: *What do I do about my rejection? What does it mean about me? What about my fear of being rejected in the future?* Remember there is hope. Your fear of rejection can diminish or vanish. It is possible, especially when your hope is in the person of Jesus Christ. We begin to overcome *both* the effects of a relationship rejection and the fear of a future rejection by experiencing what the ultimate source of acceptance offers us: grace in Jesus Christ.

THE TRANSFORMING POWER OF GRACE

Grace can simply be defined as a free gift from God that results in giving you significance and value at a new level. Grace is God's kind disposition, unconditional love, concern, compassion, and favor toward you, no matter the circumstance—yes, no matter the situation. The greatest gift of his grace was given to us through Christ.

Because of Christ's redemption,

I am a new creation of infinite worth,

I am deeply loved,

I am completely forgiven,

I am totally pleasing,

I am totally accepted by God,

I am absolutely complete in Christ.

When my performance

Reflects my new identity in Christ,

That reflection is dynamically unique.

There has never been another person like me

In the history of mankind,

Nor will there ever be.

God has made me an original,

One of a kind,

A special person.[6]

Read these statements out loud each day for a week and discover the difference these true statements will make in your life and how you will see yourself. You will indeed have a new identity.

DEALING WITH ANGER

Expressions of anger have always been with us. We find anger expressed in the Bible—particularly in the psalms and the books of the prophets. Job expressed anger at God, as did Jonah and Elijah. Jeremiah cried out:

> *You deceived me, LORD, and I was deceived; you overpowered me and prevailed. I am ridiculed all day long; everyone mocks me. Whenever I speak, I cry out proclaiming violence and destruction. So the word of the LORD has brought me insult and reproach all day long.*
>
> — Jeremiah 20:7–8

Anger is a sign of protest—a reaction against something that shouldn't have happened.[7] It's a way of fighting back when you feel helpless. And it is a normal response to feeling as if you've been unjustly deprived of something valuable, in this case a close and meaningful relationship.

At whom do we get angry most often? God. We blame him. He shouldn't have done this, or he shouldn't have allowed that. We prayed about this relationship and asked him to guide us. He's supposed to do things right, which means according to the way we want!

When you blame God, it's unnerving and unsettling to other people, so they either respond with Christian clichés or try to convince you that your anger at God is irrational. They fail to realize that nothing they say will help, because you're living on emotions at this point. Even though you may be raising questions, you're not really looking for answers. The good news is that when anger is expressed to God, it can be analyzed and dealt with, and it can lead to a rediscovery of the character and purposes of God.

Your anger may also be directed toward other people, especially the ex-partner It's not uncommon for ex-partners to bad-mouth each other. Sometimes ex-partners do this so much that others wonder what the two of them ever saw in each other. Why do you, a rejected person, begin to talk about your ex in such a negative manner? It's because of loss. You hurt. You've been hurt. You tend to talk about the negative aspects of your ex-partner, so you can think of the loss as an *acceptable* loss. By focusing on the negatives of what you leave behind, it's easier to walk away from it.

Taking Inventory of Your Hurts[8]

Perhaps the initial step in overcoming anger with one's ex-partner is to take inventory of the hurts. List your hurts as if you were speaking to your ex. One person wrote:

➢ I was so angry at you for the lies.

➢ I resent the fact that I have to change churches. It should be the other way around for what you did.

➢ I feel wounded by your betrayal of me. We had talked about marriage, but you were straying even then.

➢ I am angry that you took two years of my life.

Making such a list is *not* an easy experience. Often, when a person begins listing these resentments, buried hurts and feelings climb through the barriers. This list is for your own use and is not to be shared with anyone else except God. Sharing with others can bring unsolicited comments. Let God be the provider of comfort and strength.

After you've made your list, go into a room and set up two chairs facing each other. Sit in one chair and imagine the other person sitting opposite you, listening to what you are sharing. Read your list aloud with your tone and inflections reflecting the feelings you have. Don't be concerned about editing what you are saying. Just get it out.

Some people keep their list for days, adding to it as things come to mind. Others find it helpful to sit down and share like this several times for the benefits of multiple episodes of emotional drainage. Don't be surprised to find yourself feeling angry, depressed, intense, embarrassed, or anxious. When you have concluded your time of sharing, spend a few minutes in prayer sharing these feeling with God, thanking him for understanding what you are experiencing and for his presence in your life to help you overcome the feelings.

Venting at Others

Sometimes your anger is vented toward anyone who is around, especially family members. You may get angry at those who fail to reach out and support you during this time. Friends, coworkers, and family may not know what to say, and may choose to hang back and be silent. Often they do so out of respect for your privacy, and they don't want to pry.

But when we hurt, we want to be acknowledged. We don't want people to pretend everything is okay, because it isn't. And in some cases it will never be the same.

You may direct your anger inward. Women are more likely to do this, while men generally turn anger outward. Often anger comes because we feel out of control, powerless, and victimized. Sometimes, other people genuinely are compassionate. You can ask those friends to listen to you put the pain in words. Reassure them you will get past it eventually, but expressing it to another person is part of the healing.

Releasing Anger

How do you deal with anger in a positive way? You admit it, you accept it, you release it in a healthy way. A friend of mine wrote the following poem. Maybe you can relate.

I Told God I Was Angry

I told God I was angry.
I thought He'd be surprised.
I thought I'd kept hostility
quite cleverly disguised.

I told the Lord I hate Him.
I told Him that I hurt.
I told Him that He isn't fair,
He's treated me like dirt.

I told God I was angry
but *I'm* the one surprised.
"What I've known all along," He said,
"you've finally realized."

"At last you have admitted
what's really in your heart.
Dishonesty, not anger,
was keeping us apart.

Even when you hate Me
I don't stop loving you.
Before you can receive that love
you must confess what's true.

In telling me the anger
you genuinely feel,
it loses power over you,
permitting you to heal."

I told God I was sorry
and He's forgiven me.
The truth that I was angry
has finally set me free. [9]

FINDING HOPE IN THE CRISIS

Before ending this chapter, I'd like to tell you about a woman who came into my office the second week after the breakup of her four-year relationship. She said:

> I'm just not myself. I'm doing things I've never done before and I just hate it. I wouldn't want anyone to know how irrational I am right now. You know what I've done this week? I can't believe it. I followed cars and even people that I thought were my ex. Of course they weren't. I've also called some mutual friends to find out subtly whether they've heard anything or talked to my ex or if he's seeing anyone. I guess I wasn't that subtle either.
>
> Yesterday I drove to my ex's work and apartment. I called from pay phones, so the number couldn't be traced. I just wanted to hear his voice. I know it's over, but I keep hoping. I have some of his things, but if I send them back, it will seem so final. I keep hoping, even though I know it's over. When I think

of all that wasted time, I get a pain in my stomach. I've had a headache, can't eat and when I do, it doesn't stay with me. . . . What's wrong with me?

Nothing was wrong. All that she said is part of a normal initial response to a breakup. It's natural to resist the fact that the relationship is over. When you lose someone significant, you don't want to let them go, so you hang on in any way that you can. You even do things you think are irrational, and this makes you think you're going crazy. These acts of desperation are only a problem if they persist. What will help you to move ahead is to grieve, say goodbye, and cry—again and again, if necessary.

For many, a breakup is a crisis. It's a time when you've been thrown off balance. You're confused, you can't think straight, you cry every day, and your emotions are in disarray. What you want most is relief. But there's something else. A breakup is a time when you'll make some of the greatest changes in your life. You will come out of it a better, stronger person than you were before.

CHAPTER TWO

The Recovery Process

S o how do you recover? The first thing to do is face what has happened to you. You may not like what happened, you may not even understand why it happened, but accepting it does not mean liking it. If you deny you're in pain, you're stuck.

You will hurt. Pain is the natural result of loss, especially when a dream dies. When there's a hole in your life, pain fills it for a time. This is normal.

HAVING A TIMETABLE

You probably have a timetable for recovery, and if your timetable is like that of most people, it is not realistic.

You'd like to be over the pain right now—today—this moment. Instant recovery simply does not happen in real life. There's no quick fix for emotional pain. A big part of your life and even your identity has been cut off. And contrary to what other people might have you believe, this is not a minor injury; it can be a deep, serious wound. Dick Innes, in *How to Mend a Broken Heart*, says:

> Nature has its own time schedule. You can't push it. A scratch heals in a few days. A broken bone takes six weeks. You can't speed either one up, but you can take good care of the wound, doing what you can to facilitate its healing and letting nature take its course by giving it the time it requires to heal.

> The same principle applies to healing wounds of the heart. You can't speed up the process, but you can stop it from taking longer than necessary—by taking good care of yourself, doing what you can to facilitate your healing, and giving yourself permission to take time to heal.[10]

The recovery time of a breakup is directly related to three factors:

1. How long you were involved in the relationship.

2. How close the two of you were.

3. How you perceive the chances of finding someone else.

Obviously, the first factor is clear: the longer a person had been with a partner, the longer the person would need to recover from the breakup. But what about the second factor? How can a person tell how close he or she was to an ex-partner? The longer you were involved, the closer you were likely to be. You had more shared experiences and perhaps more dreams that have now been shattered. As for the third factor, the future, if you think that you'll never find someone else or that no one will want you, you'll end up feeling stuck. After breaking up, it's best not to think about future relationships for a while. That will come later, after the healing process.

People experience a lot of confusion at the beginning of the grieving process, so be patient. Avoid making major decisions that can be put off for a few months, when your mind is clearer. Push the delay button. Write out your feelings. Write out your prayers. If it's a difficult day, call a friend and ask them to pray for you. Above all, do not begin any new relationships for several months or as long as it takes to recover. After all, would you want to begin a relationship with someone who was mourning over a former partner? And don't try to numb the pain with alcohol, drugs, or sex.

Getting over a breakup is in many ways like a car that has stalled and needs to sit awhile before it moves on. Years ago, when cars had the old-style carburetor, there would be a vapor lock. This shut down the engine, and you just had to wait. The engine didn't need a major overhaul or even a minor tune-up. It just needed to cool down until it got back to normal. And it did. Just like you will. While you wait, please remember: your options are *not* closed. As this door closes, many new ones open.

CLEANING UP MEMORY LANE

You've got to want to let go of your past life with this person. Your emotions and their intensity are related to memory, and there are different variations of memory. As Henri Nouwen put it: "Remorse is a biting memory, guilt is an accusing memory, gratitude is a joyful memory, and all such emotions are deeply influenced by the way we have integrated past events into our way of being in the world. In fact, we perceive our world with our memories."[11] What are *your* memories right now?

Have you ever considered the possibility that much of the suffering of a person's life comes from memories? The reason they hurt is because such memories tend to be mostly buried and emerge only when they choose. The more painful these memories are, the more hidden and repressed they become. They hide, as it were, in a corner of the deepest cavern of our minds. Because they are hidden, they go unhealed.

When a relationship is over, what you have left are the memories. A common response when there's a loss of this type is to idealize the person you lost. You think only of the positive qualities that you are going to miss rather than being objective. Keep in mind, the more you idealize the person, the longer your recovery is delayed. Some have found it helpful to complete a Relationship Balance Sheet, which consists or a list of positives about the relationship beside a list of problems the relationship had. Why not take some time to fill out a Relationship Balance Sheet right now?

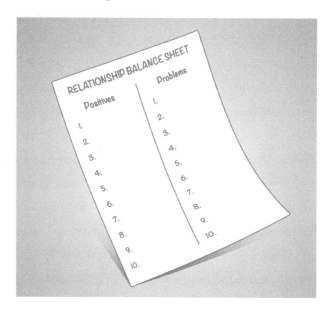

When it comes to a failed relationship, many people end up listing more problems than positives, and it is important for a person who is mourning the end of a relationship to see this.

There are also relationships where the problems can't fully be identified. There may not have been any friction or arguments. Some individuals just don't want to continue in a relationship. They don't see a future together.

What do you do with a painful memory? You may try to forget it, or you may act as though it did not occur. Trying to forget the pains of the past gives these memories power and control over your life, and you proceed through life, dragging their weight. You attempt to edit your own personal history by choosing what to remember and what to forget, but there is a twofold cost: You continue to limp through life, and you miss out on an opportunity to grow and mature. But it doesn't have to be this way.

A painful memory can be transformed into a blessing, but the first step is to face the memory. Henri

Nouwen points out: "What is forgotten is unavailable, and what is unavailable cannot be healed."[12] When you face each memory, ask yourself, *Why was this a problem? Why was this painful? What did I or can I learn from this experience?* This is a way to put the memory to rest. I've known some who have written goodbye letters to each memory and then read the letter aloud. This too can be a helpful way to let go of painful memories.

PLACING A DOWN PAYMENT ON YOUR EMOTIONAL DEBT

From time to time we all accrue emotional debt—when we trap feelings inside and block off our capacity to feel or when we fail to express our emotions. But the more we create a barrier around our feelings, the more constricted we become. Hurt is a part of life. Being let down is a part of life. We live in an imperfect world, so getting hurt is bound to happen from time to time.

Getting out of emotional debt involves accepting yourself and others, shortcomings and all. If you are guarding your emotional life, you're under continuous stress, and your vision of reality is clouded. No matter how painful your past experiences have been, no matter how much you want to remain at a safe intellectual distance from your pain, healthy people need to both think and feel.

People who stuff their feelings often detach themselves from others. This detachment is born out of fear, and these people live in constant fear. For them, fear is like a soft hum in their ears, reminding them to be cautious and wary.

If any of this is hitting close to home, consider these questions: What is it you are afraid of? If you have a good, trustworthy confidant, what is the worst possible thing that could happen to you if you opened your life to your feelings? Would it be any worse than what you are experiencing now?

If you want to live life in the present, with hope for the future, accept what has happened in the past, for it cannot be changed. If you are lonely, share your feelings with someone who cares about you and can connect with you emotionally. If you are sad, tell someone. By doing so, you'll be placing a down payment on your emotional debt.

CARING FOR YOUR CHILDREN

When a family with children dissolves because of a divorce, the family that the children knew dies. If you have children, you're well aware of this experience. Fortunately, more than ever before, a lot of attention is being given to the impact of divorce on children. Unfortunately, very little attention is given to the impact of a single parent's breakup on children. In some cases, the ending of a long-term dating relationship by a parent can be even more devastating than divorce for children.

Your children's responses to your breakup may include sadness, abandonment, isolation, confusion, disorientation, and anger. They may worry that you will stop loving them. They may worry that their other parent will stop loving them. They need time and attention to feel important. When you begin to date, your children may become jealous of the time and attention you are focusing on the new person. As the innocent victims of a parental breakup, your children have a point of view that is reasonable and justified and needs to be heard. This doesn't mean you give up dating, but it does means that you give regular reassurance to your children that they are important to you. And you back that reassurance up with time and attention.

When you date, sometimes your children will compare the new person in your life with the old person, try to change loyalties and balance of power, share family secrets with the new person, and perhaps tell their other parent about the two of you.

Your children may resist your efforts to have an ongoing relationship with this individual and may take steps to sabotage your dreams to have a life with this new individual.

In many cases, because your children have lost one parental figure, they could be especially needy, quickly attaching to any new partner of yours. Just remember, *the greater the attachment, the greater the loss when there's a breakup*. You might be glad a relationship is over and feel little grief. But your small children could be crushed. If you don't allow and help them to grieve this loss (and it will take longer than you think and want), there will be long-term damage. Don't leave your children out of the picture. Talk with them, listen, reflect, and be patient. Help them grieve by taking some of the steps you've taken.

EXPERIENCING GRIEF[13]

Grieving is an active process of confronting loss and doing what needs to be done with it to move on with life. When you live in denial, however, you push anything unpleasant out of your life. In denial you passively float down a river of pain, but at the same time, you don't admit the pain is there.

> Grieving is an active process of confronting loss.

You're floating along often at the mercy of the current. Grieving admits and faces the pain. It sets a course, notes the currents and rapids in the river, and paddles through it all to maintain its course.

Grief is *not* despair. Grief feels and deals with loss. Despair is a sense of futility—the idea that nothing can be done to get out of this. It's a passive resignation, and it grinds you into hopelessness.[14]

When grief enters your life, you enter a valley—a valley of shadows. There is nothing pleasant about grief. It's painful. It's work. It's a lingering process. But it's necessary for healing.

Grief brings many changes. It appears differently at various times, and it flits in and out of your life. It's natural, normal, and predictable; and it should be expected when your relationship is over. Don't let anyone tell you that something is wrong with you. Grieving is not an abnormal response to a breakup. In fact, just the opposite is true. The *absence* of grief is abnormal. Grief is your own personal experience and does not have to be accepted or validated by others.[15]

A Bundle of Emotions

There is a bundle of emotions involved in the grieving process, emotions that seem out of control and in conflict with one another. At different times you may experience bitterness, emptiness, apathy, love, anger, guilt, sadness, fear, self-pity, and helplessness.

During your time of grief and recovery, you'll experience a jumbled mess of feelings that will leave you wondering, *Am I normal or crazy?* This in itself is normal and to be expected. One minute you're confused and the next you've got it all together. Confusion will be a companion that comes and goes. You'll be sentimental at times, especially when thoughts and mementos trigger your sadness. Your feelings will surge back and forth like a wave coming into shore and out again. You're likely to vacillate from dwelling on your ex-partner to blocking out all thoughts of the person.

Physical and Social Effects

Your entire body experiences your grief—your physical wellbeing reflects your feelings, thoughts, and attitudes. You experience grief physically as it affects your health and is expressed in bodily symptoms. If you wonder where that migraine came from or why your stomach is off, ask your grief. This physical effect, in turn, impacts you socially as you interact with others.

One of the best descriptions I've found of the overall effects of grief is from the book *The Phoenix Phenomenon* by Joanne Jozefowski, a psychotherapist who specializes in bereavement therapy:

The "crazy" feelings [of grief] are actually a *sane* response to grief. Reflect on the following examples—all symptoms of normal grief:

> ➢ distorted thinking patterns, "crazy" and/or irrational thoughts, fearful thoughts

> ➢ feelings of despair and hopelessness

> ➢ out of control or numbed emotions

> ➢ memory lags and mental "short-circuits"

- changes in sensory perceptions (sight, taste, smell, etc.)

- inability to concentrate

- obsessive focus on the loved one

- losing track of time

- increase or decrease of appetite and/or sexual desire

- difficulty falling or staying asleep

- dreams in which the deceased seems to visit the griever

- nightmares in which death themes are repeated

- physical illness like the flu, headaches or other maladies

- shattered beliefs about life, the world, and even God[16]

I would add two more characteristics to the list:

- increased irritability

- the desire to talk a lot or not at all

Necessary Changes

Why do people suffering from a breakup have to go through the experience of grieving? What's the purpose? Keep these things in mind:

> ➢ Through grief you express your feelings of loss.

> ➢ Through grief you express your feelings about the effects of the loss.

> ➢ Through grief you express your anger with the loss as well as your desire to change what happened.

The purpose of grieving is to get beyond these reactions, so you can move on with your life. Grieving will bring you to the point of making necessary changes, so you can live with the loss in a healthy way. It's a matter of beginning with *Why did this happen to happen to me?* and moving to *How can I learn through this experience?* When the how question replaces the why question, you have started to live with the reality of the loss. Why questions reflect a search for meaning and purpose in loss. How questions reflect your search for ways to adjust to the loss.[17]

Letting Go

One of the biggest steps of the grieving process is letting go of your ex. But what does letting go in a relationship mean? Here are several possibilities:

1. It means making a clear and firm decision to end your involvement with memories. After you've faced them, felt the pain, said goodbye, and released them, it's time to move on.

2. It means taking responsibility for the decision to let go and knowing that it is the right thing to do.

3. It means making a promise to yourself that the relationship is over.

4. It means making it clear to your ex-partner by your actions that it's over.

5. It means sticking by this decision, no matter how painful the process.

Guard yourself; be sure you stay away from your ex-partner. Any thoughts you have of getting your ex to take you back need to be dropped. I've seen some people plead and beg for a partner to come back. This is where the rational part of you needs to override your emotions. Think about it: would you really want to be with someone whom you had to prod into a relationship with you? Would you want to go through life telling others, "Aren't I the fortunate one? I talked my partner into accepting me and taking me back?" I don't know anyone who would, and I doubt you would either.

If you run into the other person socially, don't cower and hide or slink away. Be pleasant, positive, and brief. If your ex wants to stay and talk or explain more, don't. Give yourself permission to say no, talk with someone else, or leave the area. You need your space, your separateness, and your self-esteem.

When it comes to letting the past go, you have three choices: (1) reliving the past, (2) becoming fearful, or (3) moving ahead. Even though it's impossible to go back and relive your life, I know a number of people who have made the choice to live in the past rather than the present. They never let go of the past and thus can't move forward.

Others I've seen deal with their pain and resolve it, but they are so scared of future commitments that they stay where they are, stuck, and don't move ahead.

The healthiest choice is the third one. Once you've let go of the past, you can move ahead: take wisdom-based risks, be willing to love again. Dick Innes says that life can only be understood by looking backward, but it must be lived by looking forward.[18] God's purpose for your life is not in your past but in your future, and to go ahead you'll need to grieve and then let go.

CHAPTER THREE

Evaluating Your Progress

A friend of mine asked, "How do I know I'm getting over this breakup and recovering in the way I need to? It's been four months now, and at times I feel different and other times I don't. What's normal, or is there a normal?" Have you asked similar questions? We want to know when recovery will happen and how we will recognize it. We want an accurate self-evaluation.

Although there are various ways to tell how or whether you're progressing through recovery, keep in mind that the tools and indications for determining progress vary from person to person; the last thing you want to do is compare yourself with others.

When you find yourself thinking and talking less and less about the relationship, you're progressing. What percentage of your time do you feel at peace about your breakup, and what percentage of your time do you feel anxious about it? If you find times of balance between peace and anxiety, you're progressing. It's important that you experience a balance in your memories as well, when you remember both the good as well as the problem times.

During the initial period after a breakup, concentration comes with difficulty. So if your concentration is improving, that too is progress. Also it's a good sign when you begin to be more patient with the rate of your recovery. Most people are too hard on themselves, berating themselves for, in their estimation, taking "too long" to make progress. In fact, people often start dating just to prove to themselves that they are moving on, not to actually begin a new relationship.

TAKE TIME FOR A CHECKUP

It may be time to check where you've been and where you are today. The following are some exercises designed to help you see how much you've progressed.

Overall Condition

On a scale from zero to ten (zero being complete devastation and ten being complete recovery), evaluate where you were three months ago compared to where you are now by circling one of the numbers (if the breakup was less than three months ago, rate your emotional condition at the time of the breakup).

Three Months Ago

0   1   2   3   4   5   6   7   8   9   10
Complete devastation   Complete recovery

Today

0   1   2   3   4   5   6   7   8   9   10
Complete devastation   Complete recovery

Depression or Sadness

Another sign of recovery is when your depression or sadness begins lifting and you start enjoying life a little. Depression or sadness still may come and go, but if it seems to have less of a grip on you, recovery is on the horizon. How would you characterize your level of depression or sadness today? Circle the statement that comes closest to describing your level of low feelings:

➢ Depression or sadness seems to cloud my whole life.

➢ I'm just beginning to face the cause of my unhappiness and do something about it.

➢ I'm confronting my low feelings and beginning to break free.

➢ I'm moving out of my depressed or sad state.

➢ I'm enjoying life.

Anger

You're recovering when you begin to take the energy of your anger and use it to move forward. You're getting a handle on your anger when you realize its source is hurt and fear. Circle the statement that most accurately describes your level of anger:

> ➤ I've not felt anger yet.

> ➤ I'm just beginning to understand the anger part of my recovery.

> ➤ I'm right in the middle of dealing with my anger.

> ➤ I've already processed my anger.

Sometimes anger is directed at different people to varying degrees. Circle the degree to which you're angry with yourself, God, and your ex-partner:

Anger at Yourself

A lot	Some	Comes and goes	Not much

Anger at God

A lot	Some	Comes and goes	Not much

Anger at Your Ex

A lot	Some	Comes and goes	Not much

Ability to Function

Another sign of recovery has to do with ability to function. A friend shared with me a few months after her breakup:

> I'm starting to be functional again. It's not a chore to do the necessities of life again. For a while it was so difficult to crank myself up to do even simple maintenance tasks. I can laugh again, I'm not paranoid about what I listen to on the radio or watch on TV. I used to be on edge and get upset. Not now. It seems like I took a vacation from enjoyment for a while.

I actually enjoyed looking at flowers the other day and went into a florist shop and bought some . . . for me! I'm also working out again. I love to run and even though I got out of shape and I'm sore, I'm running again. And that's helping my appetite. Food tastes better than ever now.

Isolation

Did you isolate yourself after the breakup? Many do. They don't want to be around others. But it seems that close friends are needed for recovery. Isolating yourself just brings you down. So although mere acquaintances may drain you, you need to push yourself to connect with the people who nourish your soul. As you begin to recover, others move from being draining to being energizing. And that's as it should be. But it's a process, and it probably won't happen as fast as you want.

MAKE ADJUSTMENTS FOR RECOVERY

Have you ever been in the hospital for an operation? If so, you know the procedure. After the operation is over, you're taken to a recovery room. You stay there for a few hours until the effects of the anesthetic begin to wear off. The term *recovery* is a bit misleading for this room. It certainly doesn't mean total recovery. It actually means helping you adjust to the effects of the operation, so you are ready for the real recovery, which will take time. Dr. Ann Stearns, professor of psychology, compares recovering from a loss to traveling on a highway:

> Recovery from loss is like having to get off the main highway every so many miles because the direct route is under reconstruction. The road signs reroute you through little towns you hadn't expected to visit and over bumpy roads you hadn't wanted to bounce around on. You are basically traveling in the appropriate direction. On the map, however, the course you are following has the look of shark's teeth instead of a straight line. Although

you are gradually getting there, you sometimes doubt that you will ever meet up with the finished highway.[19]

Recovery doesn't mean a once-and-for-all conclusion to your loss and grief. It is a twofold process involving the reduction and eventually the elimination of pain associated with the breakup as well as the renewal of your ability to function normally in your day-to-day life. But recovery includes something else too: change. Your loss changes you. As someone

The solution is to move forward.

once asked in a counseling session, "If I can't be the way I was before this breakup, what is all this talk about recovery? What does it mean? How can you recover, yet not return to your old self?" The question is not so much how you can recover without going back to your old self. The question is whether you'll ever recover if you're focused on going back to who you were before the breakup. No, the solution is to move forward, to allow your breakup to shape you so that you are stronger and wiser for the experience.

I have a scar from a childhood operation. When I see it, I'm reminded of the operation. A breakup leaves an internal scar, and as with some physical scars, this breakup is in such a sensitive place that you're likely to feel a twinge of pain now and again. There's no predicting when these twinges will come. Only for a fortunate few, however, is recovery complete, so the former relationship is a distant memory and no twinges come.

Recovery includes reinvesting in life, looking for new relationships and new dreams. But you could very well feel uncomfortable with whatever is new; that's not unusual. You may have questions and concerns, because your previous experience didn't turn out the way you thought it would. If you begin to hope or trust again, it's possible you will experience another breakup.

Recovery includes reinvesting in life.

Do you realize that you have a choice in your recovery? Most don't have a choice in their loss, but everyone has a choice in their recovery. You have a choice about whether you will be affected positively or negatively by the breakup.

I've talked to those who have chosen to live in denial and move through life as though nothing happened. I have talked to people who have been stuck in the early stages of their grief who have chosen to live a life of bitterness and blame. They hated members of the opposite sex. "They're all the same" was a common refrain. Some became so hardened and angry that it was difficult to be around them for an extended period of time. They were not pleasant. If they've continued in this pattern for years, they've made a choice to be a permanent victim and to demonize others. They seem to have forgotten that life is full of losses, and we have the choice to do something constructive or destructive with the losses that come our way.

Evaluate Your Wellness[20]

You can gain a sense of how your recovery progress is going by evaluating the changes in yourself, the changes in your relationship with the person you lost, and the changes you have made to adjust to your new world. As you take and review the following evaluations, the conclusions you reach may help you determine where you are in your recovery and how far you have to go. But before you begin, I'd like to encourage you to go through these evaluations with a good friend who can assist you with an objective viewpoint. Sometimes another person is the difference between a distorted view of reality and a clear view of reality.

For each evaluation, use a scale from zero to ten (zero meaning "I disagree entirely" and ten meaning "I totally agree") to rate your level of agreement with each statement.

The Changes in Myself

I have returned to normal levels of functioning in most areas of my life.

0 1 2 3 4 5 6 7 8 9 10

Disagree entirely   Totally agree

My overall symptoms of grief have declined.

0 1 2 3 4 5 6 7 8 9 10

My feelings do not overwhelm me when I think about my loss or when someone else mentions it.

0 1 2 3 4 5 6 7 8 9 10

My anger has diminished, and when it occurs, it is handled appropriately.

0 1 2 3 4 5 6 7 8 9 10

Most of the time I feel all right about myself.

0   1   2   3   4   5   6   7   8   9   10

I enjoy myself without feeling guilty.

0   1   2   3   4   5   6   7   8   9   10

I don't avoid thinking about things that could be or are painful.

0   1   2   3   4   5   6   7   8   9   10

I have the ability to think positively.

0   1   2   3   4   5   6   7   8   9   10

My ex-partner does not dominate my thoughts or my life.

0   1   2   3   4   5   6   7   8   9   10

I believe there is meaning and significance to my life.

0   1   2   3   4   5   6   7   8   9   10

I see hope and purpose in life, in spite of my loss.

0   1   2   3   4   5   6   7   8   9   10

I have energy and can feel relaxed during the day.

0   1   2   3   4   5   6   7   8   9   10

I can handle special days or dates without being totally overwhelmed by memories.

0   1   2   3   4   5   6   7   8   9   10

I can remember the loss on occasion without pain and without sadness.

0   1   2   3   4   5   6   7   8   9   10

I no longer fight the fact that the loss has occurred. I have accepted it.

0 1 2 3 4 5 6 7 8 9 10

I am learning to be comfortable with who I am now as a single person.

0 1 2 3 4 5 6 7 8 9 10

I understand that my feelings over the loss will return periodically, and I can understand and accept that.

0 1 2 3 4 5 6 7 8 9 10

I understand what grief means and have a greater appreciation for it.

0 1 2 3 4 5 6 7 8 9 10

The Changes in My Relationships with the Person I Lost

I remember our relationship realistically—with both positive and negative memories.

0 1 2 3 4 5 6 7 8 9 10
Disagree entirely   Totally agree

I don't feel compelled to hang on to the pain.

0 1 2 3 4 5 6 7 8 9 10

The relationship I have with the person I lost is appropriate.

0 1 2 3 4 5 6 7 8 9 10

My life has meaning, even though my ex is not a part of my life.

0 1 2 3 4 5 6 7 8 9 10

The Changes I Have Made to Adjust to My New World

I am open about my feelings in other relationships.

0   1   2   3   4   5   6   7   8   9   10
Disagree entirely   Totally agree

I feel it is all right for me to go on, even though my ex has left me.

0   1   2   3   4   5   6   7   8   9   10

I have developed an interest in people and things outside of myself that have no relationship to the person I lost.

0   1   2   3   4   5   6   7   8   9   10

I have put the loss in perspective.

0   1   2   3   4   5   6   7   8   9   10

AVOID GETTING STUCK

Sometimes as you try to recover from a broken relationship, you end up getting stuck, like a car stalled on the side of the road. There are some warning signs, however, that will let you know whether you're stuck.

One warning sign is an inability to accept what has happened.[21] I've talked to some people who just wouldn't accept what had happened. One woman said, "He was just upset. I know he didn't really mean it. He'll be calling soon." The pain of facing the loss is too much, so they hold on to a "togetherness fantasy."

Another warning sign is isolation from others. This will happen to some degree, even if you're not stuck, but it should not go on endlessly. For some, withdrawal is selective. For others, it's total. If you withdraw for too long, the isolation begins to feed on itself, and the grief will grow rather than decrease.

Some people seem to stop living. They quit eating, quit going to work, quit doing all the things that people normally do. At first this may be expected, but as an ongoing pattern, it's a warning sign. June, a single mother of two, shared:

> At first, my two children understood, but after several months they'd had it. They told me I looked terrible, and they were tired of making their own lunches. When they said they needed me to be their mom again, I heard them. In two weeks I buried my ex-partner emotionally, quit neglecting myself, and then got back into life.

A very real problem for many is a dependence on alcohol or drugs. It's a way to find short-lived relief and comfort, and when it's over, the user does not go back to life as usual; he or she feels worse. I've known some people who never used drugs and alcohol before a breakup and then plunged into substance abuse afterward. Drugs and alcohol do not solve grief; they prolong it.

Thinking or talking obsessively about the breakup is also a sign of being stuck. If you've ever been around someone like this, it probably wasn't for long. Why?

People who do this demonstrate little progress in their recovery. They have a one-track mind, and others grow tired of hearing the same old song. If you don't seem to be able to move past the grief, you may need a support group or one-on-one counseling with a professional who will understand. The more you think or talk about the loss with people who have never walked in your shoes, the more the pain is intensified. It's like hitting yourself again and again in the same place. There's constant damage. And there's little energy left for moving on.

Take Control of Your Situation[22]

What can you do if you're having a difficult time moving forward? The following suggestions will help you take control of your situation:

1. *Try to identify what it is that doesn't make sense to you about your breakup.* Perhaps it is a vague question about God's purpose in this. Or it could be a specific question (e.g., *Why did this have to happen to me now, after all the time I invested?*). Ask

yourself, *What is it that is bothering me the most?* Keep an index card with you for several days to record your thoughts as they emerge.

2. *Identify the emotions you feel during each day.* Are you experiencing sadness, anger, regret, hurt, or guilt? What are the feelings directed at? Has the intensity of the feelings decreased or increased during the past few days? If your feelings are vague, identifying and labeling them will diminish their power over you.

3. *Identify the steps or actions you are taking to help you move ahead and overcome this breakup.* Identify what you have done in other relationships that helped you, or ask a trusted friend for help.

4. *Be sure you are sharing your loss and grief with others who can listen to you and support you during this time.* Don't look for advice givers but for those who are empathetic and don't mind listening to what you have to say.

5. *Find a person who has experienced a similar loss.* It would be helpful to find or help organize a Relationship Recovery Group similar to a Divorce Recovery Group. Reading books or stories about those who have survived similar experiences can be helpful.

6. *Identify the positive characteristics and strengths of your life that have helped you before.* Which of these will help you at this time in your life?

7. *Spend time reading the Psalms.* Many of them reflect the struggle of human loss but give the comfort and assurance that are from God's mercies. See Psalms 34:6; 46:1; 138:3; and 147:3.

8. *When you pray, share your confusion, your feelings, and your hopes with God.* Be sure to be involved in the worship service of your church, because worship is an important element in recovery and stabilization.

9. *Think about where you want to be in your life two years from now.* Write out some of your dreams and goals. Just setting some goals may encourage you to keep moving forward.

10. *Remember that understanding your grief intellectually is not sufficient.* It can't replace the emotional experience of living through this time. You need to be patient and allow your feelings to catch up with your mind. Expect mood swings, and remind yourself of these suggestions through notes placed in obvious places. Mood swings are normal.

Recovery is a back-and-forth process. One of the best ways to mark your progress is through a personal journal. This will give you proof that you are making progress, even though your feelings say otherwise. Your journal is your own private property and is not for anyone else to read—don't blog or post your journal writings online. It is an expression of what you are feeling and your recovery climb. It can be written in any style: simple statements, poems, or prayers that reflect your journey. The authors of the *Grief Adjustment Guide* offer some helpful suggestions for a journal:

1. You may find it helpful to make time every day to write at least a short paragraph in your journal. At the end of a week, review what you have written to see small steps of progress toward grief recovery. Writing at least a line or two every day is the most effective way to keep a journal.

2. Some people write in their journals a few times each week, reviewing them at the end of the week and at the end of each month.[23]

If you have trouble getting started, look over the following list of suggested beginnings from Dwight Carlson and Susan Carlson Wood, the authors of *When Life Isn't Fair*. Find one that fits what you are feeling or need to express, and use it to jump-start your writing for the day:

1. My biggest struggle right now is . . .

2. The thing that really gets me down is . . .

3. The worst thing about my loss is . . .

4. When I feel lonely . . .

5. The thing I most fear is . . .

6. The most important thing I've learned is . . .

7. The thing that keeps me from moving on is . . .

8. I seem to cry most when . . .

9. I dreamed last night . . .

10. I heard a song that reminded me of . . .

11. A new person I've come to appreciate is . . .

12. I get angry when . . .

13. Part of the past that keeps haunting me is . . .

14. What I've learned from the past is . . .

15. Guilt feelings seem to come most when . . .

16. The experiences I miss the most are . . .

17. New experiences I miss the most are . . .

18. The changes I least and most like are . . .

19. My feelings sometimes confuse me because . . .

20. I smelled or saw something today that reminded me of . . .

21. A new hope I found today is . . .

22. New strengths I've developed since my loss are . . .

23. I feel close to God today because . . .

24. I am angry at God today because . . .

25. For me to find and have balance, I . . .

26. I got a call or letter from a friend today that . . .

27. My friend, _____, had a loss today, and I . . .[24]

If one of those doesn't fit, then write about what you are feeling. You could start with just one word (*misery*, *longing*, or *hope*, for example) and then describe that feeling with phrases or sentences. If you need to, cry as you write, but keep writing until there is nothing more to say about that feeling.

Your journal is yours to say and feel what is in your heart and mind. It is your way of crystallizing the feeling of loss. Dealing with your feelings one at a time in a written, tangible form is a good way to own your feelings and respond to them in an organized way.

Grief involves a tangle of feelings.

Grief often involves a tangle of feelings; writing them down is a great way to isolate and experience catharsis with each one.

Monitor what you write. When you begin to write more about what is happening *today* and less about the person you have lost, you'll know that healing and adjustment are indeed taking place. Though the process may seem painfully slow, look for signs of progress.[25]

THE SLIPPERY SLOPE OF RECOVERY

Thomas Whiteman and Randy Peterson, the authors of *Fresh Start: 8 Principles for Starting Over When a Relationship Doesn't Work Out*, warn of the dangers of rebound relationships:

> When an arm breaks, it's put into a cast—immobilized so that no more damage is done as it heals. You need to do the same thing with your heart. Beware of rebound relationships. Protect your heart. Put it in a cast until it can heal.
>
> Granted, this is hard to do. You have unmet needs—socially, physically, spiritually. You feel as though there's a gaping hole in your gut, and you want to fill it *now*. With that kind of pressure, you can make awful decisions. *Who cares if the person shares your values, your interests, your faith? It's a warm body!*

Rebound relationships of any sort are more likely to hurt you than help you. Not only are such relationships shortsighted and based on desperation, but they also set you up for additional injury.[26]

The authors go on to explain how the process of recovering from relationship trauma is similar to a teambuilding exercise involving a muddy pit:

Two teams of students [were] put into a muddy pit. The goal: Get your whole team out and keep the other team in. Of course the whole business got pretty messy. Just when you thought you were safely out of the pit, some enemy would pull you back in.

And that's exactly how it works when you are getting over a relationship trauma. You think you're out of the pit, but your "enemies"—reminders, doubts, worries, or perhaps the people who put you down to begin with—keep dragging you down again.

The Slippery Slope
POINT OF TRAUMA

Old Lifestyle — New Lifestyle

Denial

Anger — Forgiveness

Bargaining

Depression — Acceptance

While the slippery slope is common in all grieving situations, it is especially prevalent when a person rushes through the grief. When we hurry through the stages, it's likely that something will trip us up.

God does give us peace, but it usually comes at the end of a process that takes a couple of years. We can cite case after case of people who took their healing slowly, and they have become much stronger, more mature believers. *This* is the best testimony to God's healing power.[27]

Perhaps you feel as though you're on a slippery slope or you've been on it for a while. Most people have been there. And you will slide back down the slope. Every slide is called a relapse. Relapses are normal, and as strange as this may seem, if you have relapses, it's an indication that you're recovering, even if it doesn't feel like it. Here are some relapse triggers:

➤ When you begin looking at how far you have to go to recover and you get overwhelmed.

➤ When you feel you're different from other sufferers (or should be) and become overconfident.

➤ When you see someone who reminds you of your former partner or when you actually run into your ex.

When you fall down the slope the first time, it's hard to get back up. But it's easier after falling, because you've been there and know how to climb out.

What triggers you to slide down the slope? If you can identify what it is, you may be able to anticipate and even prevent a few slides. If not, you may at least be aware of what's coming.

Debrief Your Old Relationship

I hope you are at a place in your recovery where you can complete what I refer to as a relationships debriefing. By doing a debriefing, you will learn even more about yourself and future relationships. Feel free to write your answers in a journal.

1. What were your initial thoughts and responses to your ex when you first met?

2. What do you think ex's initial reaction to you was like? What did he or she think? Did the two of you ever discuss your initial reactions?

3. If you weren't that interested at first, what brought about the change? Has this been a pattern in your relationship?

4. At the beginning of the relationship, who did the pursuing? Did this pattern continue throughout the relationship?

5. Were both you and your partner available for a permanent relationship?

6. Throughout a relationship, feelings can change and fluctuate. What were your feelings at various stages? Circle the number that best reflects your feelings at the time.

At the Beginning of the Relationship

0   1   2   3   4   5   6   7   8   9   10

Negative   Neutral   Average   Very positive   Love

At the Middle of the Relationship

0   1   2   3   4   5   6   7   8   9   10

Negative   Neutral   Average   Very positive   Love

At the End of the Relationship

0   1   2   3   4   5   6   7   8   9   10

Negative   Neutral   Average   Very positive   Love

7. If feelings changed at times, what were the causes?

8. How would you chart your ex's feelings for you at the various stages? Use the scales above, but draw a box to indicate your ex-partner's level of affection.

9. When the relationship started, did you have any reservations? If so, what were they? Did your friends have any reservations? If so, what were they? Did your family have any reservations? If so, what were they?

10. What do you wish you knew about your ex at the beginning of the relationship that you do know now?

11. How would this have made a difference?

12. What didn't your ex-partner know about you at the beginning of the relationship that could have made a difference?

13. What do you wish you would have done differently?

14. In what way did you discuss problems in the relationship?

15. Who brought up the problems? Who was most resistant to discussing problems? Did the discussions bring about positive changes?

16. How did the relationship end? Who ended it? Who resisted and how?

17. What might have made this relationship work?

18. What are your thoughts and feelings about your ex at this time?

19. What specifically did you learn from this experience that will help you in the future?

20. What are some reasons that your breakup was ultimately for the best?[28]

CHAPTER FOUR

Moving Ahead

L isten to the words of a twenty-four-year-old
counselee of mine:

> It's hard to be alone again. It's been two years
> since I've been single. I guess you hope that each
> relationship will turn into a lasting one, but when
> I've been contented with being alone, but not this
> time. I feel lonely . . . and it hurts.

ACCEPT LONELINESS AS A TEMPORARY VISITOR

Loneliness—a feeling with many dimensions. It's
feeling that you don't matter, that you've been cut

off from others. Loneliness is when you feel isolated, deserted, or even banished from relationships with others. It's feeling that even though you're in a room full of people, you're still all alone. The word itself has a mournful and eerie sound. It is cold like the earth in winter when the birds and flowers have abandoned it.

The clue to what loneliness is really like can be found in Psalm 142:4: "No one cares about me" (GW).

People in the Bible experienced loneliness. In their separation from God, Adam and Eve were the first to experience loneliness. Even Jesus felt the pangs of loneliness. He was misunderstood by many and only partially understood by his disciples. He suffered loneliness in the Garden of Gethsemane, in Pilate's judgment hall, and on the cross (see Matthew 26– 27). Jesus' heart was full of love for his people, so it's no wonder he felt lonely. His love was rejected.

> Loneliness is a season... It doesn't last forever.

Perhaps the words of David are your words: "[Lord,] turn to me and be gracious to me, for I am lonely and afflicted" (Psalm 25:16).

It's normal to feel lonely now and then. That's not a problem. The problem begins when we feel lonely constantly, and I've seen this in some of the most gregarious, personable men and women you could ever meet.

Loneliness arises when the relationship you once had becomes the central focus of your life. Life revolves around one person, who is no longer present. It seems as though there's nothing left to hang on to. And if your partner is the one who called it quits, you have the additional pain of rejection.

Loneliness can lead to a state of being frozen— you want love, but the fear of reaching out to accept the love that friends might offer can limit you from supportive relationships. Loneliness arises when your focus is on what you lost, and you forget about friends or the potential for making friends.

Loneliness is a season that you'll go through as someone who is newly single again, but remember what a season is like. It's short. It doesn't last forever.

At first it may seem overwhelming and unmanageable, but it should lessen after a few months. Loneliness is a part of grief, so as you grieve, the feeling of loneliness will lift, even without a significant person in your life.

Loneliness is a regular part of life when you have relationships. To be completely free from the risk of loneliness, a person would have to lead a life in which no one he or she ever cared about was lost or absent.

The feeling of loneliness is like the feeling of depression. Feeling depressed is not the problem. But feeling depressed alerts you to a problem. It tells you something is wrong, and you need to discover what's wrong and take the appropriate steps to fix it. It's uncomfortable, but it prompts you to take action. If you give in to loneliness and let it take up residence in your life, you suffer endlessly. If instead you play host to loneliness as a temporary visitor whom you encourage to be on its way, then you move on in life.

CHOOSE ACTIVE SOLITUDE

The first thing to realize is that you have a choice between sad passivity or active solitude. The first consists of doing nothing, wandering through your home aimlessly, sleeping, drinking, overeating, taking tranquilizers, watching TV, or using drugs. This leads to a downward spiral from emotional and social isolation to depression. But in active solitude, you engage in constructive activities such as exercise, painting, reading, taking a class on the Internet, or helping and serving others.[29] It's your choice.

Be selective in your friendships and relationships. If you're lonely, admit it. But before searching for people to fill the need, consider this: what would you do if you were isolated on an island for years like the character played by Tom Hanks in *Cast Away*? How would you fill your life? If you have a personal relationship with Jesus Christ, make the most of it. Talk with him. Read his Word. Spend time in fellowship with healthy Christians. Look for ways to serve God in ministry.

Do you have a close friend who can be a prayer partner? This kind of person would be like-minded and could hold you accountable to the Lord.

Too many who are single have said they need to be in a relationship or be married in order to be happy or fulfilled. But this sounds more like dependency than anything else. Authors and licensed psychologists Henry Cloud and John Townsend point out: "If you are afraid of aloneness and abandonment, you cannot use the love of people who are truly there until you deal with your own fears. So, aloneness must be cured first."[30] Many believe, *When I am accepted by another, I will be satisfied and my life will be fulfilled*. But being accepted by another person or gaining another person's approval never leads to permanent satisfaction.

If you are addicted to the acceptance and approval of another person, there is a high price to pay. The price tag includes an extreme vulnerability to the whims and subjective opinions of the people around you. Others can take advantage of your vulnerability and mistreat you, which leads to rejection. When we seek to fulfill our lives by depending on other people's perceptions of ourselves, we shut off God's blessing and his affirmation in our daily experience.

PURSUE GOD

Years ago I heard an older counselor say, "You can't be happily married to another person unless you're happily married to yourself." It made sense. If I don't feel satisfied with who I am, another person isn't going to solve that. My relationship with God will. He's the one who brings wholeness and satisfaction. Cloud and Townsend explain:

> Have a full life of spiritual growth, personal growth, vocational growth, altruistic service, hobbies, intellectual growth and the like. The active growing life does not have the time or inclination to be dependent on a date. The more you have a full life of relationship with God, service to others, and interesting stimulating activities, the less you feel like you need a relationship in order to be whole.[31]

Cloud and Townsend go on to say:

> In addition to an active life, work on the issues that are in your soul. Whatever those issues are (past childhood hurts, recurring themes and patterns in your relationships and work life, and other areas of brokenness, pain, and dysfunction), your aloneness will be cured as well. It is a curious thing, but the process of spiritual growth itself can help cure aloneness. As you grow spiritually, you are going to naturally grow closer to others and gain a fuller life. . . .
>
> The best boundary against giving in to bad relationships . . . is your not needing that relationship. And that is going to come from being grounded in God, grounded in a support system, working out your issues, having a full life, and pursuing wholeness."[32]

Some individuals make the pursuit of a marriage

partner their life goal. But the pursuit of a relationship with God is much more fulfilling. Listen to the psalmist: "I sought the LORD, and he answered me; he delivered me from all my fears" (Psalm 34:4).

When you pursue God, the pain of not having your ex-partner in your life diminishes. I've seen God take away not only the *pain* of a broken relationship but also the fear of never finding a marriage partner.

Singles tell me they are looking for a mate who can really help them walk with God. But if you need a romantic partner to help you know God intimately, you have misunderstood the Christian faith. Your walk with God is a personal relationship with him expressed through fellowship, hospitality, and community with other believers in Christ. It is not meant to be a vicarious, secondhand relationship through a boyfriend or girlfriend. Each of us is responsible for our own walk with the Lord.

Instead of looking for the right person, focus on a responsible, reliable person. Don't shape yourself to fit some imaginary partner's criteria.

Have you ever considered that God can give you a quality of life right now that is better than anything you could ever create with another person or on your own? It's worth considering.

Have you ever thanked God for where you are in your life right now? Perhaps you're not ready yet. You may be in too much pain. But showing gratitude to God is a way to relieve the pain. One common way of doing this is to write a list of twenty things you're thankful for. Begin this process and you may be amazed at the results.

DON'T GIVE UP ON NEW RELATIONSHIPS

The thought of dating again can be exciting—and scary. One minute you're daydreaming about Mr. or Ms. Right, and the next minute you see and hear a relationship disaster hovering in your future. This combination of fantasy and fear affects many people as they contemplate the brave step of reentering the dating world.

Your first few dates may not be the best experiences. You might be on edge and feel awkward. You might be expecting the worst or be on your guard too much. The signals you're likely to give off will be a mixture of curiosity and reluctance: "I'm interested, but keep away." Your emotional wounds may not yet have turned into scars. Don't worry. All of this is normal, so don't give up.

Be Cautious

Scripture warns again and again to be on your guard. Listen to these warnings: "Only be careful, and watch yourselves" (Deuteronomy 4:9); "be careful to do what the Lord your God has commanded you" (Deuteronomy 5:32); "be careful to obey all that is written in the Book" (Joshua 23:6). Being careful means to be wary, to keep your eyes open, to be alert. Let your guard down once, and you may do something that will cause great harm.

Don't Date Someone You Don't Know

Spend your time getting acquainted and building a relationship with a new someone. Don't even call it dating. Who wants to date a stranger? Clarify your expectations and boundaries right from the beginning.

The best romantic relationships grow out of friendships. It's also much easier to relax and be yourself in the beginning of a dating relationship, if the person you date is already a friend.

Realize What You Can and Can't Control

I've heard both men and women say some variation of the following: "One of the things that holds me back from entering a new relationship is the fact that I can't control the outcome." That's true. You can't control what's going to happen, nor can you control the other person's feelings about what may happen, nor can you control the other person's feelings toward you. So my advice is to give yourself permission to be without control in those areas. What you can control is your own responses to the other person, so make sure your responses are in line with your feelings. Don't send mixed signals. Don't move too quickly. Be cautious, with both your own heart and with the heart that belongs to the person you're dating.

Identify Your Fears

How has fear played a part in your relationships? Have you ever been in a relationship in which you wanted to connect with the other person, but you were afraid to move ahead? Or perhaps it was your partner who wanted to reach out to you but was immobilized by fear. The important thing is to identify which fears affect you, so you are aware of them. Once you've identified them, then you can evaluate whether your fears are valid.

Don't Fall for Myths

I've seen many singles cripple their relationship's potential by believing myths. Myths, in this sense, are inaccurate beliefs, generalized as gospel truth, based on the negative experiences of a small number of people.

Has anyone ever told you this myth: "There aren't enough eligible partners out there"? Another relationship myth is summed up by this statement: "I'll never find the kind of person I really want, so why bother?" Another myth may sound familiar: "I'm too old to start looking, let alone dating." Who put time limits on looking and dating? Only you can do that. I regularly encourage singles in their sixties, seventies, and eighties to keep dating. One more myth is related to the loser mentality: "I'm a loser and that's all I'll ever find." Or you may be familiar with a similar defeatist attitude: "All the good ones are taken."

An important thing to remember when dating is that you will meet some people who are more compatible with you than others, but you will never find a perfect person. The only place perfect people exist is in our minds.[33]

Beware of Rebounding

Relational rebounding is when a person goes immediately from one relationship to another without taking time to heal from the end of the first. Often the rebounder is in intense pain and instead of experiencing the loss and grief on his or her own, the rebounder tries to cover some of the pain by entering a new relationship.

If you enter a new relationship with a load of pain,

your hurt is likely to distort your perception of the other person, and it will be difficult in this state to make an emotional connection. Rebounding hinders the rebounder from healing and contaminates any new relationship. Both people need to be stable and healthy for a relationship to have a chance.

In a potential new relationship, you may want to look for clues to how similar or dissimilar you are to his or her former partner. I have seen many people choose men or women who are just like their former partners, defects and all.

Before any person can move ahead with a new relationship, it's necessary to say goodbye to the former relationship. It's the final step of grieving over a relationship.

Stay Away from Prebounders

There is a second kind of person who is hazardous to relational health. I've heard this kind of person referred to as a prebounder. Prebounders are very similar to rebounders except they are still involved in one relationship while they look for a new one. Prebounders are looking for a safety net to fall into once the current relationship fails.

Avoid Bad Candidates

Sometimes courtship problems arise because a person becomes involved with an individual who is just not a good candidate from the outset. Some relationships have such large barriers to begin with, they will never survive.

One of the interesting factors I've come across in years of counseling singles is how often a person will be drawn to a person who is unavailable in one way or another. Sometimes the person is already involved with another individual. Some are geographically unavailable. Some are unable to commit. Some have a bad character: they are liars, irresponsible, addicted, angry, selfish, or mean. Not everyone is good marriage material.

Remember as you move ahead: Every relationship we have is either a *depleting* or a *replenishing* relationship. A depleting relationship is one in which you are with someone who drains you emotionally and spiritually. The relationship taps your energy reserves in some way. It can happen in long-term dating relationships or in a marriage. Being around this type of person is just plain hard work. At first the relationship may seem workable, but soon it becomes an exercise in coping. Those who deplete you contribute to your problems rather than help you resolve them.

You don't want a depleting relationship—in any kind of situation. You want replenishing relationships—relationships with people who energize and vitalize you. They add to your life in a positive way; and remember—one of the best ways to draw people like this is to be this kind of person yourself.[34]

Yes, breakups are difficult. But every painful experience in our lives provides the opportunity to change, grow, and become more Christ-like.

Notes

1   Much of this section is from H. Norman Wright, *Finding the Right One for You: Secrets to Recognizing Your Perfect Mate* (Eugene, OR: Harvest House Publishers, 1995), pp. 44–45.

2   Zev Wanderer and Tracy Cabot, *Letting Go: A 12-Week Personal Action Program to Overcome a Broken Heart* (New York: Dell Books, 1987), pp. 11–12.

3   Stephen Gullo and Connie Church, *Loveshock: How to Recover from a Broken Heart and Love Again* (New York: Simon and Schuster, 1988), p. 26

4   For more detailed information about breakup in relation to family and friends, please see Diane Vaughan, *Uncoupling: Turning Points in Intimate Relationships* (New York: Oxford University Press, 1986), pp. 140–47

5   Much of this section is from Wright, *Finding the Right One for You*, pp. 46–47.

6   Robert S. McGee, *The Search for Significance* (Nashville, TN: W Publishing Group, 1998, 2003), p. 266.

7   What follows in this section is based on Vaughan, *Uncoupling*, p. 42–43.

8   Much of this section is from Wright, *Finding the Right One for You*, pp. 55–56.

9   Jessica Shaver, "I Told God I Was Angry" Posted June
     20, 2010, first published in *Time of Singing*, May 1989,
     His Scribe Downloads Blogspot http://hisscribedownloads.
     blogspot.com/2010/06/poem-i-told-god-i-was-angry.html

10   Dick Innes, *How to Mend a Broken Heart: 20 Active Ways*
     to Healing (Grand Rapids, MI: Baker Book House,
     1994), p. 36.

11   Henri J. Nouwen, *The Living Reminder: Service and Prayer*
     in Memory of Jesus (New York: HarperCollins, 1977),
     p. 19.

12   Ibid., p. 22.

13   Much of this section is from H. Norman Wright,
     Recovering from Losses in Life (Grand Rapids, MI:
     Fleming H. Revell, 2006), chapter 2.

14   Scott M. Stanley, *The Heart of Commitment: Cultivating*
     Lifelong Devotion in Marriage (Nashville, TN: Thomas
     Nelson, 1998), pp. 80–88.

15   Therese A. Rando, *How to Go On Living When Someone*
     You Love Dies (Lexington, MA: Lexington Books, 1988),
     pp. 11–12.

16   Joanne T. Jozefowski, *The Phoenix Phenomenon: Rising*
     from the Ashes of Grief, rev. ed. (Northvale, NJ: Jason
     Aronson Inc., 2001), p. 17.

17 Bob Diets, *Life After Loss: A Personal Guide Dealing with Death, Divorce, Job Change, and Relocation* (Tucson, AZ: Fisher Books, 1988), p. 27

18 Innes, *How to Mend a Broken Heart*, p. 47.

19 Ann Kaiser Stearns, *Living Through Personal Crisis*, 2nd ed. (Enumclaw, WA: Idyll Arbor, Inc., 2010), p. 86.

20 Much of this section is from Wright, *Recovering from Losses in Life*, chapter 7.

21 Much of what follows in this section is based on Aleta Koman, *How to Mend a Broken Heart: Letting Go and Moving On* (Lincolnwood, IL: Contemporary Books, 1997), pp. 177–82.

22 Much of this section is from Wright, *Recovering from Losses in Life*, pp. 80–81; 122–23

23 Charlotte A. Greeson, Mary Hollingsworth, and Michael Washburn, *The Grief Adjustment Guide: A Pathway Through Pain* (n.p.: Queststart Publishers, Inc., 1990), n.p.

24 Dwight L. Carlson and Susan Carlson Wood, *When Life Isn't Fair: Why We Suffer and How God Heals* (Eugene, OR: Harvest House, 1989), p. 38.

25 Ibid., p. 43.

26 Thomas Whiteman and Randy Peterson, *Fresh Start: 8 Principles for Starting Over When a Relationship Doesn't Work* (Wheaton, IL: Tyndale House, 1997), pp. 83–84, 100–103, 113–15.

27 Ibid.

28 Steven Carter and Julia Sokol, *He's Scared, She's Scared: Understanding the Hidden Fears That Sabotage Your Relationships* (New York: Dell, 1993), pp. 172–74.

29 Jacqueline Olds, Richard Schwartz, and Harriet Webster, *Overcoming Loneliness in Everyday Life* (New York: Carol Pub. Group, 1996), pp. 119–20.

30 Henry Cloud and John Townsend, *Boundaries in Dating: How Healthy Choices Grow Healthy Relationships* (Grand Rapids, MI: Zondervan, 2000), p. 73.

31 Ibid., p. 74.

32 Ibid., pp. 74–75.

33 For more information about dealing with new relationships, see Tina Tessina, *The Unofficial Guide to Dating Again* (New York: Wiley Publishing, Inc., 1998), chapter 2.

34 For more information about depleting and replenishing relationships, see Ronnie W. Floyd, *Choices: Making Sure Your Everyday Decisions Move You Closer to God* (Nashville, TN: Broadman and Holman, 1994), pp. 70–74.

Other titles by Dr. Norm Wright

Discovering Who You Are and How God Sees You

When we know who we are in God's eyes, our confidence won't allow the ups and downs of life destroy our self-worth. Releasing our dependence on having the right job, the right posessions, and hanging out with the right people will bring us a deeper sense of peace and satisfaction that no disappointment can take away.
ISBN 9781628620504

Helping Your Hurting Teen

Is your teen withdrawing, acting unusual, sullen or distracted? Do you feel like you just don't know your child anymore? Are you afraid it's more than just a stage? Learn which responses are "normal" adolescent behaviors, and which ones indicate deeper issues related to loss or trauma. Expert Dr. Norm Wright gives insight on how to reconnect with your child, understand their struggle, and never lose hope. **ISBN 9781628620542**

Overcoming Fear and Worry

When anxiety robs your sleep, when worry saps your energy, and when fear captivates your thoughts, it is easy to feel helpless. But you do not have to remain a prisoner of fear, anxiety, or stress any longer. Dr. Norm Wright helps you combat negative thought patterns with the Word of God and gives you practical ways to develop resilience in the face of trials through positive self-talk.
ISBN 9781628620627